Discover Birds

by Victoria Marcos

© 2014 by Victoria Marcos
ISBN: 978-1-62395-636-3
eISBN: 978-1-62395-640-0
ePib ISBN: 978-1-62395-641-7
Images licensed from Fotolia.com
All rights reserved.
No portion of this book may be reproduced
without express permission of the publisher.
First Edition
Published in the United States by Xist
Publishing
www.xistpublishing.com
PO Box 61593 Irvine, CA 92602

Birds are found on every continent of the world.

Ibises are large birds found in wetlands over wide areas throughout South America and the Caribbean islands.

Most ibises make their nests in trees, often living with other birds.

Ibises use their long curved bill to dig for food in the mud.

Flamingos live in several different warm coastal areas throughout the world.

They are born grayish-red and later turn light pink to bright red, depending on how much bacteria is in their food.

Flamingos eat brine shrimp and blue-green algae.

Herons are freshwater and coastal birds found almost everywhere except in the coldest environments.

They have long necks that they can form into an S-shape.

Herons use their long sharp bills to catch fish.

7

Canada geese live in very cold regions of North America and the Arctic.

When they migrate, they fly in large flocks in a V-shape.

Canada geese are mostly herbivores but, sometimes they eat insects and fish.

Seagulls are seabirds that live on the shorelines of every continent.

They feed on fish as well as anything they can find on land.

Seagulls are intelligent and resourceful birds, sometimes working together to gather food.

Parrots live in tropical and subtropical regions throughout the world.

They eat mostly nuts, seeds, fruit, and flower buds.

They are colorful, highly intelligent birds. Some species have the ability to imitate, or copy, human voices and other sounds.

Yellow-crested cockatoos are found on a few areas of East Timor and two Indonesian islands.

They live mostly in mountain forests, but also live mangroves and plantations.

Yellow-crested cockatoos eat mostly fruit, nuts, seed and flower buds.

15

16

Toucans are native to Southern Mexico, Central America, and the northern part of South America and the Caribbean.

They live in forest and make their nests in tree hollows.

Toucans mostly eat fruit, but will also eat insects and small lizards.

Emperor penguins are the tallest of all penguins and live only in Antarctica.

They can't fly but, are excellent swimmers.

Emperor penguins eat fish, crustaceans, and cephalopods.

Ostriches are native to certain parts of Africa and Asia Minor.

Like penguins, ostriches can't fly. However, they can run over 40 miles per hour.

Ostriches mostly eat grass, seeds, fruit, flowers, and sometimes eat locusts.

Peafowl are mostly known as "peacocks." The males are called peacocks, the females are called peahens and the chicks are called peachicks.

They live in parts of Asia and Africa.

They are omnivorous forest birds that eat plants, insects, and reptiles.

Storks can be found in Africa, Asia, and Europe. There are a few species that can be found in Australia and between Florida and Argentina.

They make large nests in high places.

Storks eat fish, frogs, insects, worms, small birds, and small mammals.

Griffon vultures live mostly in Asia, Southern Europe, and North Africa, making nests in cliffs far from humans.

They are large birds with wingspans of over nine feet.

Griffon vultures feed mostly from carcasses of dead animals they find while flying high above open areas.

Eagles are large, powerful birds of prey found in the United States, Canada, Central and South America, Australia and New Guinea.

Their eyesight is almost four times better than that of humans. This helps make them excellent hunters.

Eagles will eat any kind of meat and also fish.

The bald eagle lives in North America and is the national bird of the United States.

They're not actually bald. The name means "white headed."

Bald eagles live near water and mostly eat fish. They swoop down and grab fish with their talons.

American crows live in most parts of North America.

Crows are very intelligent birds. They can recognize humans, use tools, and have been known to use bait to catch fish.

They eat almost anything they can find.

33

Barn owls are found mostly everywhere except near the north and south poles, deserts, parts of Asia and some Pacific Islands.

They are nocturnal. During the day they sleep in quiet, hidden places.

They mostly hunt for land animals during the night.

www.ingramcontent.com/pod-product-compliance
Lightning Source LLC
LaVergne TN
LVHW021600070426
835507LV00014B/1886